W9-CPG-884

SPECIAL REPORTS

RUSSIAN HACKING IN AMERICAN ELECTIONS

BY DUCHESS HARRIS, JD, PHD WITH MARCIA AMIDON LUSTED

Essential Library

An Imprint of Abdo Publishing | abdobooks.com

abdobooks.com

Published by Abdo Publishing, a division of ABDO, PO Box 398166, Minneapolis,
Minnesota 55439. Copyright © 2019 by Abdo Consulting Group, Inc. International
copyrights reserved in all countries. No part of this book may be reproduced in any
form without written permission from the publisher. Essential Library™ is a trademark
and logo of Abdo Publishing.

Printed in the United States of America, North Mankato, Minnesota
092018
012019

Cover Photo: Boonchai Wedmakawand/iStockphoto
Interior Photos: Rogelio V. Solis/AP Images, 4–5; Bob Andres/Atlanta
Journal-Constitution/AP Images, 9; Andrew Harnik/AP Images, 11; Julie Jacobson/AP
Images, 13; AP Images, 14–15, 24; Universal History Archive/Universal Images Group/
Getty Images, 20; AFP/Getty Images, 27; Patrick Semansky/AP Images, 28–29; Paul
Holston/AP Images, 32; Alexei Nikolsky/Sputnik, Kremlin Pool Photo/AP Images, 36; J.
Scott Applewhite/AP Images, 38–39; Richard Drew/AP Images, 41; Marcy Nighswander/
AP Images, 44; Rawpixel.com/Shutterstock Images, 48–49; FLDphotos/iStockphoto, 51;
Jon Elswick/AP Images, 53; Steve Marcus/Reuters/Newscom, 54; Jose Luis Magana/
AP Images, 56; Eve Edelheit/Tampa Bay Times/AP Images, 62–63; Tom Williams/CQ
Roll Call/AP Images, 65; Evan Vucci/AP Images, 69; Shutterstock Images, 70; Rich
Pedroncelli/AP Images, 72–73; Bebeto Matthews/AP Images, 78; Alexandr Piragis/
Sputnik/AP Images, 80; Pablo Martinez Monsivais/AP Images, 83; Alex Wong/Getty
Images News/Getty Images, 84–85; Andrew Harrer/picture-alliance/dpa/AP Images,
88; Mark Wilson/Getty Images News/Getty Images, 91; Adam Gerrard/Daily Mirror/
Newscom, 94–95; Seth Wenig/AP Images, 96

Editor: Alyssa Krekelberg
Series Designer: Maggie Villaume

Library of Congress Control Number: 2018948247

Publisher's Cataloging-in-Publication Data

Names: Harris, Duchess, author. | Lusted, Marcia Amidon, author.
Title: Russian hacking in American elections / by Duchess Harris and Marcia
    Amidon Lusted.
Description: Minneapolis, Minnesota : Abdo Publishing, 2019 | Series: Special
    reports set 4 | Includes online resources and index.
Identifiers: ISBN 9781532116827 (lib. bdg.) | ISBN 9781532159664 (ebook)
Subjects: LCSH: Presidents--Election--Juvenile literature. | Election monitoring--
    Juvenile literature. | Computer hacking--Juvenile literature. | Russian Far East
    (Russia)--Politics and government--Juvenile literature.
Classification: DDC 327.73047--dc23

CONTENTS

CHAPTER ONE

ELECTION DAY
2016

I t was November 8, 2016—Election Day in the United States. All over the country, polls were open. People were voting for the presidential candidate of their choice: Donald Trump, the Republican candidate, or Hillary Clinton, the Democratic candidate.

Most of the polls that had taken place preceding the election seemed to indicate that Clinton would win by a wide margin and that Trump did not stand much of a chance of becoming president. As late as 8:00 p.m. on election night, polls still showed a 78 percent chance that Clinton would win and only a 21 percent chance of Trump winning.[1]

In 2016, millions of people voted on Election Day.

A SURPRISE UPSET

The predictions of a big victory for Clinton faded as the night went on. Trump began to win state after state. In the early morning hours of November 9, Clinton called Trump to congratulate him and to concede the election. President-elect Trump tweeted, "Such a beautiful and important evening! The forgotten man and woman will never be forgotten again. We will all come together as never before."[2]

A few hours later, Ken Thomas of the Associated Press tweeted, "Russian President Vladimir Putin sends Donald Trump a telegram of congratulation on winning the US presidential election."[3] It may have seemed like an innocent message from the Russian leader. But in this case, the communication between Putin and Trump strengthened some people's suspicions that Russia had meddled in the 2016 US election. It also underlined the pro-Russian attitude of President-elect Trump.

It would later be revealed that the US intelligence agencies, acting on a request from President Barack Obama, had discovered that Russian operatives had compromised the state websites or voter registration databases in seven states: Alaska, Arizona, California, Florida, Illinois, Texas, and Wisconsin. The investigation also revealed that Russian operatives had been involved in the hacking of emails of US political figures and institutions. Following the investigation, the Obama administration released a public statement about the Russian interference. The administration took measures to punish Russia. This included sanctions and the expelling of Russian diplomats from the United States.

Some sources argued about the accuracy of the information revealed by the intelligence investigation. However, in September 2017, the US Department of

GRACEFUL DEFEAT

On November 9, 2016, the day after the election, Clinton gave a speech conceding the presidential race to Trump:

Last night, I congratulated Donald Trump and offered to work with him on behalf of our country. I hope that he will be a successful president for all Americans. . . . I know how disappointed you feel because I feel it too, and so do tens of millions of Americans who invested their hopes and dreams in this effort. This is painful and it will be for a long time, but I want you to remember this. Our campaign was never about one person or even one election, it was about the country we love and about building an America that's hopeful, inclusive and big-hearted. We have seen that our nation is more deeply divided than we thought. But I still believe in America and I always will. And if you do, then we must accept this result and then look to the future. Donald Trump is going to be our president. We owe him an open mind and the chance to lead.[4]

Homeland Security also stated that as many as 21 states may have had their voting systems infiltrated to some degree.[5]

Some states experienced difficulties on Election Day. In North Carolina, some voters found themselves facing many problems. Some people were told that they were ineligible to vote, even when they had current registration cards. Others were sent from one polling place to another and were still denied the ability to vote. And some people were told incorrectly that they had already voted earlier that day.

Most of the state's voting problems could be traced to the fact that electronic databases had replaced paper voter registration lists. VR Systems is a company that provides voter registration systems to state and local officials. It had provided some of the software for those databases. And the company had been accessed months earlier by hackers. The National Security Agency (NSA) believed the hackers were working for Russian military intelligence. Similar voting problems had also occurred in Virginia, Georgia, and Arizona.

Some people waited in long lines to vote.

US government intelligence officials reassured Americans after the election that there was no evidence that Russian hackers had altered the actual vote counts on Election Day. However, they did not offer any reassurances about the voting system itself.

NOT JUST VOTES

Interfering with voters and voting systems was just one aspect of Russian interference known as Active Measures. This is a kind of political warfare done by Russian intelligence agencies. The goal is to influence world events. Tactics during the election season included Russian operatives visiting the United States secretly. Once in the country, they conducted investigations to get information and carried out cyberattacks. They also created contacts within US political groups and institutions.

US intelligence agencies' investigators believed that Russian hackers may have enabled the release of confidential emails from the servers of the Democratic National Committee (DNC), which is the formal governing organization of the US Democratic Party, with help from organizations that publish secret information. Some of these groups included WikiLeaks and DCLeaks. WikiLeaks is a large international media organization. It was started by Julian Assange, an Australian computer programmer, in 2006. It specializes in analyzing and posting secret or censored data and documents related to war, spying, and corruption. DCLeaks was later found to be a front organization for Russian military intelligence.

These groups succeeded in highlighting the controversy about Clinton's use of a private email server for her government emails while she was the US secretary of state. Official government correspondence from officials such as the secretary of state is supposed to be hosted on government servers. This is to preserve the official documents and ensure that they are readily available to the government. Clinton was the secretary of state during part of the Obama administration, from 2009 to 2013.

After the election, there would also be increasing evidence that the Trump campaign had developed a relationship with Russia long before Trump ran for president. Evidence would also lead people to believe that the candidate's connections, and those made by his staff, would make it easier for Russian hackers and secret Russian operatives to sway the election in his favor.

REASONS WHY

But what was the reason for Russia's interest in American politics? On election night in a bar in Moscow, Russia, Trump supporters cheered as election results were

In July 2016, Hillary Clinton was investigated by the FBI over using a private email server. The investigation later said Clinton should not face criminal charges.

STRONGER TOGETHER

hillaryclinton.com

broadcast. Alexei Zhuravlyov, a Russian legislator, praised the pro-Russia position Trump had taken, saying, "This is the real reset."[7] This was a reference to a 2009 remark made by the Obama administration about "pressing the reset button" and seeking a fresh start in Russia–US relations.[8]

Throughout the campaign, Americans had become more politically divided than they had been in years. Groups representing women, science, and civil rights organized protests and marches against Trump. Many people felt that Russia had succeeded in not only influencing the US presidential election but also helping worsen political divisions. In the months following Trump's election, this division would erupt in racial violence and hate speech toward groups such as immigrants.

The day after the election, Obama tried to reassure his staff, saying, "History zigs

STAYING IN TOUCH

A few days after the 2016 presidential election, Russian spokespeople didn't deny that there were contacts between Russia and Trump's campaign. Russian deputy foreign minister Sergei Ryabkov told a Russian news agency, "Obviously, we know most of the people from his entourage. Those people have always been in the limelight in the United States, and have occupied high-ranking positions. I cannot say that all of them, but quite a few have been staying in touch with Russian representatives."[9]

Donald Trump gave his victory speech in New York at around three in the morning.

and zags. . . . It is not a straight line. A lot of what we achieved can be sustained. Don't be discouraged."[10] Many Americans were disheartened, but other people were excited about the election results. They felt that Trump would do things differently than past presidents and that he spoke for the average American.

Why did Russia seem to seek a division in the American people? The roots of its actions lie in a long history of tensions during the Cold War (1945–1991). During this era, the Soviet Union and the United States—both superpowers of the time—faced off in a struggle for military, political, and cultural dominance without ever entering a direct armed conflict.

CHAPTER TWO

A COLD WAR
LEGACY

T he United States and Russia have had a changing relationship over the past 100 years. While the two countries have often been adversaries, there have also been times when they were allies.

The United States and Russia, which was part of the Union of Soviet Socialist Republics, or the Soviet Union, were both part of the Allied forces during World War II (1939–1945). The Allied forces opposed the Axis powers, which included Nazi Germany, Italy, and Japan. However, even as part of an alliance with the United Kingdom, France, and Australia, the United States and the Soviet Union did not get along easily. The Soviet Union was what the US government called

President Harry S. Truman, *right*, met Soviet Union leader Joseph Stalin at a conference on July 17, 1945.

a Communist state, but some people note that it was actually socialist.

The United States operates under the capitalist system and was skeptical about Communism. The United States also opposed the actions of Soviet leader Joseph Stalin.

COMMUNISM VS. SOCIALISM

Communism and socialism are economic and political systems. They are similar in some ways but different in others. Communism is a system in which the working class owns everything but everyone works toward a common goal. Everyone belongs to the same class with no wealthy or poor people. Everything that is produced is distributed equally to the people, depending on need. However, it often results in poverty and low production.

Socialism, like Communism, also focuses on everyone being equal. However, the means of production are owned by the government, and people are paid wages for their work, which they can spend as they choose. Workers receive what they need to survive. However, they aren't especially motivated to produce more than the minimum required because there are no incentives for good work.

Stalin ruled his country harshly. He was known to resort to violence as a way to control his people.

On their side, the Soviets resented the fact that the United States refused to treat them as a player on the world stage. They were also angered by the fact that the United States' delay in entering World War II had possibly caused the deaths of tens of millions of Russians.

The Allies won the war in 1945, but by then the relationship between the

United States and the Soviet Union was beginning to deteriorate. Most historians mark this as the beginning of what is called the Cold War. *Cold war* refers to hostilities between countries that are carried out with threats, propaganda, and other methods, but not open armed warfare. The deterioration in US–Soviet relations would lead to decades of animosity, suspicion, and indirect conflict.

THE EARLY YEARS

When World War II ended, the Soviet Union began a process of establishing control in other Eastern European countries. It created governments that would be allied with the Soviet Union's government in Moscow. The Soviet government is often known as the Kremlin. This name comes from a fortified complex in the heart

JOSEPH STALIN

Joseph Stalin ruled the Soviet Union for more than 20 years. He helped modernize the Soviet Union and made it into a world superpower, but he was also known for the terror he brought down on his own people. Upon assuming control of the Soviet Union in 1924, Stalin rid himself of unwanted Communist Party officials as well as people suspected of opposing his government. He used tactics such as midnight arrests and showy, public trials. In the 1920s and 1930s, he seized land owned by peasants to turn into collective farms, but many peasants did not want to work for the state, and collective food production suffered. Millions of peasants died from forced labor or starved during the famine that resulted from decreased food production. Those who resisted—also numbering in the millions—were executed or sent to labor camps.

A COLD WAR

Bernard Baruch first used the term *cold war* in a speech in 1947 when he was visiting the South Carolina House of Representatives for the occasion of his portrait being unveiled. He said, "Let us not be deceived; we are today in the midst of a Cold War. Our enemies are to be found abroad and at home. Let us never forget this: Our unrest is the heart of their success."[1]

of Moscow that is a center of the government.

The Soviet Union's expansion made many Americans nervous. They feared that the Soviet Union would want to expand its influence after it controlled Eastern Europe. The United States adopted a policy of containment. This policy meant that the United States would try to prevent the Soviet Union from expanding too far and becoming too powerful.

For the first few years following the beginning of the Cold War, most of the hostilities between the United States and the Soviet Union were political, not military. They argued within the United Nations, an international organization set up after World War II to mediate conflicts and prevent another devastating war. They also tried to create closer ties with countries that had not yet committed to being allied with either side. But by 1950, the relationship between the two countries, which were now viewed as world superpowers, began to focus on military power. This was intensified by various events. One event

was the Communist takeover of China in 1949. Another

was the Korean War (1950–1953). During this conflict, the

Soviet Union supported Communist North Korea. The

United States and United Nations supported the South

Korean republic. Another event that raised tensions was

the Cuban missile crisis in 1962.

Tensions also rose with the adoption of the Warsaw

Pact defense treaty among Soviet nations and the

formation of the North Atlantic

Treaty Organization (NATO)

alliance among the United

States and its allies. The Warsaw

Pact and NATO were defense

alliances that formalized

military relationships. The

Warsaw Pact was between the

Soviet Union and seven of its

satellite states in central and

Eastern Europe. NATO included

the United States and several

North American and European

THE CUBAN MISSILE CRISIS

The closest that the world ever came to full-fledged nuclear destruction may have been during the Cuban missile crisis in 1962. Soviet premier Nikita Khrushchev had placed Soviet ballistic nuclear missiles in Cuba. Some people believed this was uncomfortably close to the US coast of Florida. President John F. Kennedy declared to the Soviet Union that the United States would not permit such weapons on Cuban soil. The result was a tense standoff that nearly led to a nuclear war before Khrushchev backed down.

countries. The alliances cemented the question of which countries would support the United States and the Soviet Union if there were military conflicts.

AN ARMS BUILDUP

As the relationship between the United States and the Soviet Union became more military focused, the countries began to build up arms. The US National Security Council said in a classified 1950 report that the biggest threat to the United States was the Soviet Union. It also noted that the only way to be prepared against this threat was a massive buildup of the US military and its weapons arsenal. As a result of the report and other indications,

The United States deployed its first nuclear bomb in 1945. It hit the Japanese city Hiroshima.

US spending on defense almost tripled between 1950 and 1953.

By 1960, both sides had created a huge stockpile of weapons, including nuclear weapons. While they were a threat to the other side, the nuclear arsenals were also supposed to deter a real military conflict through a concept that became known as mutual assured destruction. The idea was that if one side used its nuclear weapons, the other side would use its own weapons in response, and both countries would be annihilated. If neither side could win such a conflict, both would be deterred from starting one.

The nuclear escalation of the Cold War colored US domestic life as well as the government's policies. Americans built bomb shelters in their backyards. They also practiced duck-and-cover drills in schools. During these drills, schoolchildren learned to crouch underneath their desks with their heads covered. They were told to do this in the event of a nuclear bomb attack. Even the movies of the 1950s and 1960s reflected the nuclear threat. Some movie plots included mutant creatures that arose from nuclear devastation.

> "THIS NATION SHOULD COMMIT ITSELF TO ACHIEVING THE GOAL, BEFORE THE DECADE IS OUT, OF LANDING A MAN ON THE MOON AND RETURNING HIM SAFELY TO THE EARTH."[2]
>
> —PRESIDENT JOHN F. KENNEDY IN A 1961 SPEECH TO CONGRESS

The Cold War also extended into space exploration. Each side was competing with the other to prove the superiority of its political, economic, and scientific systems. It also ignited the Red Scare in the United States. The Red Scare was a widespread fear that the United States had been infiltrated by Communists that wanted to overthrow the US government. One result of the Red Scare was a US congressional investigation of supposed Communist sympathizers among government workers and private citizens. Many of those people accused lost their jobs or were forced to testify against their colleagues.

THE END OF THE COLD WAR ERA

President Richard Nixon was in office between 1969 and 1974. He attempted to relax US tensions toward the Soviet Union. However, tensions heated up again under President Ronald Reagan, who took office in 1981. Reagan believed that the spread of Communism was a threat to freedom everywhere. As a result, he provided military and financial aid to anti-Communist governments around the world.

By the mid-1980s, the Soviet Union was slowly beginning to disintegrate. Soviet premier Mikhail Gorbachev came to power in 1985. He introduced two new concepts that changed the relationship between the Soviet Union and the rest of the world. These ideas were *glasnost*, or political openness, and *perestroika*, or economic reform. Slowly, Soviet Union Communist governments were replaced with non-Communist ones. In 1989, the Berlin Wall was torn down. Berlin is the capital of Germany. The wall was a visible symbol of the Cold War— it divided Communist East Berlin and democratic West Berlin. By 1991, the Soviet Union was no more. It split into several individual nations, the largest of which was Russia.

However, the end of the Soviet Union was not the end of suspicions between the United States and Russia. Even in the 2000s, diplomatic talks between the two countries were uneasy, and there was still a nuclear threat. Russia's aggressive actions in places such as Ukraine, as well as suspected cyberattacks and infiltrations in the United States, have escalated tensions. By the late 2010s, the two

Mikhail Gorbachev dissolved the Soviet Union in 1991.

powerful countries were once again engaged in an uneasy
relationship. It was this Cold War legacy of distrust, secrecy,
and covert operations that seemed to be at play once
again in the 2016 election.

MORE TO THE
STORY

RUSSIA AND UKRAINE

Tensions between Russia and other parts of the world have increased because of some of Russia's actions. In 2013, Ukraine's economy was struggling. The country's president, Viktor Yanukovych, faced a choice: join the European Union (EU) or accept a loan from Russia and join a planned Eurasian Economic Union with them. At the time, member countries of the EU included the United Kingdom, Germany, and France. Both unions are political and economic associations.

Yanukovych chose to ally himself with Russia, sparking protests in Kiev, Ukraine. On February 20, police fired on protesters. Hundreds of people were injured, and some were killed. A couple days later, Yanukovych fled the country.

In March, President Putin took advantage of the situation and moved Russian troops into the Ukrainian region of Crimea. He then annexed Crimea, making it Russian territory. His actions sparked international outrage. As of 2018, there was still ongoing conflict between Ukrainian and Russian troops, and there was a constant threat that Russia might further invade Ukraine.

FROM THE
HEADLINES

THE RISE AND FALL OF THE BERLIN WALL

In 1945, at the end of World War II, Germany was divided into four zones. Each of these zones was to be controlled by one of the Allied countries: the Soviet Union, France, Britain, and the United States. The Soviets controlled East Berlin and East Germany. The rest of the Allied countries occupied West Berlin and West Germany.

The purpose of having these Allied countries occupy Germany was to help the country become reunified. However, in 1946, reunification agreements between the Western countries and the Soviets broke down. The Western powers wanted to merge their three zones into one. But the Soviets feared that the larger zone would have more power than theirs did. The merger took place in 1947.

The Soviets tried to push the Western Allies from the city. They began by blockading West Berlin to starve the Western Allies and get them out of the city. The Western powers carried out a campaign to keep the stranded citizens supplied with food and fuel. After more than one year of this, the Soviets lifted the

The Berlin Wall became a symbolic and physical division between Western democracy and Eastern Communism.

blockade. However, they restricted East Germany's access to the West. East Germans were fleeing to the West because there were better economic opportunities and more freedom.

To prevent the loss of East Germans to the West, the Soviet Union constructed an actual wall between East and West Germany. On August 13, 1961, it began building a wall of barbed wire and later concrete. The wall would stand until November 9, 1989, when the Cold War was coming to an end.

CHAPTER THREE

HACKING AN
ELECTION

Modern presidential elections have become big media events in the United States. They are also fiercely contested races to see who will be the country's next leader. The 2016 election was particularly competitive. This was because Obama was at the end of his second term and not eligible for reelection.

In early 2016, the two major candidates for president emerged: Clinton and Trump. As the campaigns kicked into high gear, the first warning signs had already appeared that perhaps someone was trying to interfere with the US election process.

The two presidential candidates participated in a series of televised debates during the 2016 campaign.

AN EARLY WARNING

In September 2015, the Federal Bureau of Investigation (FBI) contacted the help desk at the DNC headquarters. Special Agent Adrian Hawkins called the DNC to tell it that at least one of its computers had been infiltrated by hackers. These hackers, known as the Dukes, were a team of cyberespionage experts linked to the Russian government. The FBI already had experience with the Dukes. These hackers had been trying to access the unclassified email systems of the White House, the US Department of State, and the Joint Chiefs of Staff. The FBI was well acquainted with the cyberattackers and knew that they were a real threat.

The FBI's phone call was answered by Yared Tamene, a contractor working in tech support for the DNC. After speaking with Hawkins, Tamene scanned the DNC's computer system log-ins and also looked up the Dukes on the internet. But he admitted that he did not treat the call too seriously, even though Hawkins called him again and again over the next few weeks. This was partly because he wasn't entirely sure that the FBI call was real.

"I had no way of differentiating the call I just received from a prank call," Tamene would later say in a DNC memo.[1] As the Russian interference continued, it would become clear that the efforts were focused on discrediting Clinton and helping Trump's campaign.

A TWO-WAY STREET

After the FBI sent the DNC a new message in November 2015, it became clear that the cyberattacks were not just focused on infiltrating the DNC's server to get information. The FBI informed the DNC that one of the committee's computers was transmitting information to Russia. The DNC would later claim that the computer technician who took this call did not pass along the message to party officials that the DNC system had been breached. It was clear that hackers were not only gleaning information from the party servers but also changing the servers to send information back to Russia.

In January 2016, nothing had been done by the DNC to handle this threat. So Hawkins visited the DNC headquarters. A DNC memo states, "During this meeting, SA Hawkins showed his FBI badge to us, and shared his business card, lending some credence to his claim about working for the FBI."[2] However, despite the growing seriousness of the hacks into the DNC, neither the party nor higher-level FBI officials seemed to pursue the issue or talk about how to deal with it.

ONE SMALL TYPO

On March 19, 2016, another internet issue arose. Some experts believe this event may have cost Clinton the election. It was a seemingly innocent email from Google, advising Clinton campaign chairman John Podesta that another user had tried to access his account. Google sends alerts to users of its email service, Gmail, when it seems that someone is trying to access the user's account without authorization. The alert has a link users can click on to change their password. Podesta was concerned about the email and forwarded it to a campaign staffer, who asked their internet security person about it. The security person replied to the staffer, but he made one small typo: instead of telling her that the email was "illegitimate," he typed "legitimate" instead. "It actually got managed by my assistant, who checked with our cybersecurity guy," Podesta said. "And through a comedy of errors, I guess, he instructed her to go ahead and click on it and she did."[3]

The email was a spear phishing email. Spear phishing is when a specific individual is targeted by email by someone pretending to be from a legitimate organization, with the intention of getting the person to provide sensitive information or confidential

> "I'M NOT HAPPY ABOUT BEING HACKED BY THE RUSSIANS IN THEIR QUEST TO THROW THE ELECTION TO DONALD TRUMP."[4]
>
> **—JOHN PODESTA, OCTOBER 7, 2016**

materials. When Podesta clicked on the link to change his password, what he really did was give the Russian hacker access to all of his emails. As the campaign manager for Clinton, this meant that personal and confidential emails relating to Clinton and her campaign, as well as campaign documents, could now be accessed by the hackers and shared online. By April, the DNC staff had discovered the breach, but most of the damage had already been done. They notified the FBI and hired a cybersecurity firm called CrowdStrike. This firm was able to discover who the hackers were. The hackers were familiar to cybersecurity investigators and were known to have ties with Russia. "We've known these actors for many years. . . . There's a lot of evidence that this actor is Russian or a Russian speaker," cybersecurity expert John Hultquist said.[5] Clues such as time stamps that corresponded with the Russian

PHISHING

Phishing is a type of cybercrime. It occurs when one or many targets are contacted by email, phone, or text messages by someone who pretends to be from a legitimate organization or company. However, the person's objective is actually to lure the target into providing sensitive information, such as personal information, bank account and credit card information, and passwords. It often results in personal identity theft and financial loss. *Spear phishing* is when a specific individual is targeted with the intention of obtaining confidential materials, as was the case with Podesta's emails.

time zone and computer code written in the Russian Cyrillic alphabet confirmed their suspicions.

The stolen emails and documents began appearing online in June 2016 when a mysterious blogger known as Guccifer 2.0 began posting them. The blogger was soon joined by other online entities. WikiLeaks released a statement just three days before the start of the DNC Convention. The convention is the formal gathering of the DNC and the point where the Democratic presidential candidate is chosen. WikiLeaks said that it had obtained and would post 19,000 of the stolen emails.[6] Included was a DNC email that insulted a staffer from the Bernie Sanders campaign. Sanders was competing with Clinton to become the Democratic presidential nominee. The email also appeared to indicate that the DNC favored Clinton over Sanders instead of remaining neutral.

TRUMP ENCOURAGED RUSSIAN HACKERS

After the documents from the DNC began appearing online,

"WIKILEAKS IS A GIANT LIBRARY OF THE WORLD'S MOST PERSECUTED DOCUMENTS. WE GIVE ASYLUM TO THESE DOCUMENTS, WE ANALYZE THEM, WE PROMOTE THEM AND WE OBTAIN MORE."[7]

—JULIAN ASSANGE, WIKILEAKS FOUNDER

presidential candidate Trump publicly said that he hoped the Russian spies had successfully hacked Clinton's emails. He encouraged them to publish whatever they had found.

Trump was urging a foreign adversary to spy on a former US secretary of state. Political analysts considered that his remarks could be shown as supporting Russia and inviting a closer relationship with Putin—something that went against current US policy. It also brought up questions about Russian involvement in the campaign. However, Trump later said that his remarks were intended to get the Russians to turn over their hacked material to the FBI. Of his relationship with Russia, he added, "I would

In 2018, Vladimir Putin continued to deny Russian involvement in the DNC email hacking.

treat Vladimir Putin firmly, but there's nothing I can think of that I'd rather do than have Russia friendly as opposed to the way they are right now."[8]

On September 1, 2016, Putin was interviewed by Bloomberg News. He was asked about Russia's possible involvement in the DNC hacking. Putin denied such involvement and suggested it would be difficult or impossible to prove that Russia had been behind it, saying:

You know how many hackers there are today, and they act so delicately and precisely that they can leave their mark at the necessary time and place or even not their own mark, camouflaging their activity as that of some other hackers from other territories or countries? It's an extremely difficult thing to check, if it's even possible to check. At any rate, we definitely don't do this at the state level.[9]

The summer and fall of 2016 passed, and the November election drew nearer. During this time, questions continued about Russia's involvement in the election by way of hacking. In addition, questions surfaced about Russia's relationship with Trump.

CHAPTER FOUR

A TANGLED
WEB

O n September 22, 2016, Dianne Feinstein of the
Senate Intelligence Committee and Adam Schiff
of the House Intelligence Committee issued a
joint statement:

> Based on briefings we have received, we have concluded
> that the Russian intelligence agencies are making a serious
> and concerted effort to influence the U.S. election. At the
> least, this effort is intended to sow doubt about the security
> of our election and may well be intended to influence the
> outcomes of the election—we can see no other rationale for
> the behavior of the Russians. We believe that orders for the
> Russian intelligence agencies to conduct such actions could
> come only from very senior levels of the Russian government.[1]

The press release went on to urge Putin to

immediately call a halt to the activity, and then

Dianne Feinstein believes that Russian meddling changed the outcome
of the 2016 election.

urged Americans to "stand together and reject the Russian effort."[2]

It was one of the first public acknowledgments that there could be Russian interference with the 2016 election. Just four days later, the first presidential debate took place at Hofstra University in Hempstead, New York. The debate took place at a point in the election process when the two candidates were virtually tied in the polls. At the debate, Trump was asked about the cyberattacks on the DNC and whether they were performed by a group sponsored by Russia or by a lone hacker. Trump replied that the hackers could be from Russia, China, or somewhere else entirely.

MEANWHILE, AT TRUMP'S CAMPAIGN

There were events taking place during Trump's campaign that, in retrospect, made people suspicious that perhaps Russian interference was specifically intended to help him get elected. Trump gave his first foreign policy speech on April 27, 2016. In the audience was the Russian ambassador to the United States, Sergey Kislyak. Trump's son-in-law and campaign manager, Jared Kushner, later said he shook hands with Kislyak. This was just a small incident,

Donald Trump Jr. has been under fire for his actions during the 2016 campaign.

according to Kushner, and in itself did not seem to indicate any kind of unusual support from Russia.

However, in June 2016, Trump's son Donald Trump Jr. received an email. It came from Rob Goldstone, a music publicist whose clients included a singer named Emin Agalarov, who was Azerbaijani and Russian. The email, which was later released by Trump Jr., read:

> Emin just called and asked me to contact you with something
> very interesting. The Crown prosecutor of Russia met with
> his father Aras this morning and in their meeting offered to
> provide the Trump campaign with some official documents and
> information that would incriminate Hillary and her dealings with
> Russia and would be very useful to your father. This is obviously
> very high level and sensitive information but is part of Russia and
> its government's support for Mr. Trump.[3]

Trump Jr. set up a meeting with himself, Kushner, and Trump's campaign strategist and later campaign manager, Paul Manafort, to meet with a Russian attorney named Natalia Veselnitskaya. In June 2016, they met in New York to discuss research that a Russian source had done on Clinton. Trump Jr. later said that the meeting did not present any valuable information. But it was evidence of the campaign's willingness to work with Russia to defeat Clinton. In addition, some people say that the meeting was a violation of US campaign rules. Once the news broke that this meeting had taken place, Trump Jr. denied that his father knew about the meeting.

NATALIA VESELNITSKAYA

Russian attorney Natalia Veselnitskaya claimed to have no ties to the Kremlin. But she did reach out to the Trump family after Trump won the election, asking for help with the efforts to repeal the Magnitsky Act—the 2012 Russian sanctions the United States enacted over human rights abuses. However, as of August 2018, there was no indication that Trump and his cabinet had done anything about the sanctions.

Another incident occurred in August 2016. Journalists discovered that Manafort had not disclosed that he had received millions of dollars for political consulting work for Ukraine's pro-Russian president, Viktor Yanukovych. This event showed that someone in Trump's campaign had ties to Russian interests. Following this news, Manafort resigned as Trump's campaign chairman. In addition, in June 2018, it was also revealed that Manafort had received a $10 million loan from a Russian oligarch, Oleg Deripaska, who had close ties to the Russian Kremlin and Putin.[4]

In Russia, an oligarch is a very wealthy businessperson who holds a great deal of political influence.

A BUSINESS HISTORY

Before running for president, Trump had business dealings with Russia and the Soviet Union. These dealings started in 1987. This was not especially unusual during Russia's transition from being the Soviet Union. At that time, Russian businesspeople were eager to invest in Western real estate, and Trump had many real estate holdings in the United States. Trump tried to open one of his signature hotels in Moscow as early as 1987. He discussed the possibility with the Soviet ambassador to the United States, Yuri Dubinin.

"I'VE NEVER DEALT WITH THE RUSSIAN GOVERNMENT, I'VE NEVER HAD A RELATIONSHIP WITH THE RUSSIAN GOVERNMENT. AS I'VE SAID MANY TIMES YANUKOVYCH WAS A PRO-WESTERN, NOT PRO-PUTIN, PRESIDENT."[5]

—PAUL MANAFORT, 2016

However, between 1998 and 2012, Trump's businesses were in deep financial trouble, and he nearly went bankrupt. At the same time, many Russian oligarchs needed a safe place overseas to hide their fortunes from the crumbling Russian economy. Many of them invested in Trump's various enterprises.

Many other Russians also bought real estate from Trump—especially units in Trump World Tower in New York City and in luxury high-rise buildings in Florida that Trump owned. It is not unusual for American companies and investors to create connections with Russian people and companies. But it was unusual that someone with a known history of extensive ties and debts to Russia would then run for president of the United States. Because of

Yuri Dubinin, *back left*, was the Soviet ambassador to the United States from 1986 to 1990. He met with President Ronald Reagan in the 1980s.

Trump's long history with Russian interests, his business dealings with Russia would take on a new significance as people began investigating whether there had been collusion—secret cooperation—between his campaign and Russian interests.

DURING AND AFTER THE ELECTION

On November 8, 2016, the presidential election took place. Clinton won the popular vote, with 65.8 million votes to Trump's 62.9 million. But Trump received 306 electoral college votes to Clinton's 232, making him the next US president.[6] On January 20, 2017, Trump was sworn in as president of the United States.

After the election, the question remained whether the Russian interference had been intended to help Trump's campaign specifically or was just intended to disrupt the democratic process itself. On January 6, 2017, before Trump's inauguration as president, the office of the Director of National Intelligence issued a report on the 2016 election and its investigation as to whether there was Russian interference. The Director of National Intelligence is one of the president's advisors and is part of the US National Security Council. The report stated:

> We assess Russian President Vladimir Putin ordered an influence campaign in 2016 aimed at the US presidential election. Russia's goals were to undermine public faith in the US democratic process, denigrate Secretary Clinton, and harm her electability and potential presidency. We further assess Putin and the Russian Government developed a clear preference for President-elect Trump.... We also assess Putin and the Russian Government aspired to help President-elect Trump's election chances when possible by discrediting Secretary Clinton and publicly contrasting her unfavorably to him.[7]

The major US intelligence agencies, including the Central Intelligence Agency (CIA), FBI, and NSA, all agreed with this assessment. President Trump insisted that there was no Russian interference in his campaign whatsoever. In early 2018, Trump said that he never claimed that Russia didn't meddle in the presidential election. He went on to say that his campaign never colluded with Russia.

MORE TO THE
STORY

ROLE OF
INTELLIGENCE AGENCIES

Each US intelligence agency has its own specific purpose. The FBI is tasked with defending the United States against terrorist and foreign intelligence threats, as well as upholding and enforcing the criminal laws of the United States. The CIA collects, analyzes, assesses, and distributes foreign intelligence to help the president and government policymakers so that they can make informed decisions on things that relate to national security. The NSA also collects and analyzes data and intelligence. But the NSA specializes in data from electronic communications, emails, phone calls, and other forms of computer communications. NSA employees are experts in cryptanalysis, which is the ability to decipher coded messages, and they safeguard the United States from unauthorized access by foreign countries.

CHAPTER FIVE

TROLLING ON
FACEBOOK

One of the methods that was used by Russian hackers and possibly other foreign agents to influence the election was the social media platform Facebook. The 2016 election was marked by extreme opinions about both major candidates. Facebook and other social media platforms were a prime battleground for people to express their opinions and debate with others. One person's post could inflame other people. It could start heated discussions about respective points of view over issues such as immigration, gun control, gay rights, abortion, and other controversial topics. Sensitive subjects such as race, class, and political stances often provoked users into angry dialogues.

Facebook has millions of users across the globe.

FOUNDING FACEBOOK

Mark Zuckerberg founded Facebook in 2004 when he was a student at Harvard University. He got the idea from the student directories with photos and basic information that colleges often provided to incoming freshmen to help them get to know their peers. The company's mission is "to give people the power to build community and bring the world closer together." As of June 2018, Facebook had 1.47 billion daily active users on average and 2.23 billion monthly active users.[2]

At the same time, people could be influenced in their political thinking by other people's posts, as well as by news items that appeared in their news feeds or were shared by friends. Ads were also used to sway people's thinking. Social media plays a significant role in shaping people's opinions. According to a 2016 study by the Pew Research Center, 20 percent of social media users have "modified their stance on a social or political issue because of material they saw on social media."[1]

One of the biggest tools used for manipulating voters was the posting of fake news stories that seemed to discredit a candidate with lies and inaccuracies. In the case of Facebook users who did not question the authenticity of these news stories, experts believed that it would be relatively easy to sway their political opinions. Clinton was the target of a majority of these fake news stories, but they affected Trump as well.

When the presence of fake news stories on Facebook surfaced, at first Facebook founder Mark Zuckerberg denied that Facebook could have an influence on the election. "Personally, I think the idea that fake news on Facebook—of which it's a small amount of content—influenced the election in any way is a pretty crazy idea," he said in November 2016.[3] Investigators also discovered that many of the accounts that produced these fake news stories were illegitimate and not created by authentic Facebook users.

Mark Zuckerberg was criticized for Facebook's role in the 2016 election.

TROLLS AND ADS

Facebook eventually discovered that many of the ads on its site were paid for by a Russian company linked to the Kremlin. Ads on Facebook target users' profiles. Computer algorithms use data about people's internet activity to decide what other advertisements might interest them and then show them ads that relate to those areas. These ads are how the social media company generates revenue. By the fall of 2017, Facebook had identified more than $100,000 worth of ads created especially to target divisive issues rather than to sell a product or promote a candidate.[4]

While the ads did not refer to a specific candidate, Facebook's research found that most of the 3,000 ads focused on so-called hot-button issues such as racism, gay rights, gun control, and immigration—the same topics seen in many fake news stories. The ads ran between June 2015 and May 2017. They were linked to about 470 fake accounts and pages.[5]

Another tactic used on Facebook was one called astroturfing. This is the practice of creating a false

One Facebook site created by the Russian Internet Research Agency (IRA) was called Secured Borders. It encouraged people to kill undocumented immigrants.

grassroots movement, supposedly arising from people themselves rather than an organization, and intended to either support or oppose an issue. However, in reality this supposedly grassroots movement is actually controlled by an organization or company.

The fake accounts had been created by a Russian company called the Internet Research Agency (IRA). This company already had a reputation for using troll accounts. *Troll* is an internet slang term referring to someone who appears online and intentionally creates conflicts and arguments with the aim of upsetting people or provoking them into an emotional response. The IRA was credited with creating rogue profiles, which is a Facebook profile

Alex Stamos left Facebook in August 2018.

created with a fraudulent or deceitful intention. Those

profiles included 70 accounts on Facebook and 138

Facebook pages, according to Facebook's chief security

officer, Alex Stamos.[6]

Facebook revealed in October 2017 that an estimated

ten million people in the United States had seen ads

linked to Russian accounts, with 44 percent of them

appearing before the 2016 election. Stamos said, "The

IRA has repeatedly used complex networks of inauthentic

accounts to deceive and manipulate people who use

Facebook, including before, during and after the 2016

U.S. presidential elections. . . . We know that the IRA—and

other bad actors seeking to abuse Facebook—are always

changing their tactics to hide from our security team. . . .

We expect we will find more, and if we do we will take

them down too."[7]

In addition, Facebook found that many ads were

targeted specifically at voters in Michigan and Wisconsin—

two battleground states that were crucial to Trump's

victory in the election. Battleground states are states that

are not firmly Republican or Democratic in their politics,

where voters can easily vote either way. This makes these

states into places where candidates spend a great deal of

time and money to try to ensure that they win. The ads

used a sophisticated focus to target certain demographics

in these two states and promoted anti-Muslim viewpoints

that the creators felt would appeal to a particular group of

voters. These ads may have influenced the close election

results in these states. Trump won both Michigan and

Wisconsin by less than 1 percent of the vote.[8]

CAMBRIDGE ANALYTICA

In addition to IRA, there was another company at work

during the 2016 election that also turned out to be using

Facebook as a method for gathering data. Cambridge

Analytica was a political data company based in London. Its purpose was to harvest data from various sources to meet the needs of its clients. Cambridge Analytica had been hired by the Trump campaign. The company was to provide data to the campaign about voters and their behavior. This data could then be used to target campaign ads and other election materials.

However, it later emerged that Cambridge Analytica gained access, with Facebook's consent and cooperation, to the personal data of more than 50 million Facebook users and their friends.[9] The data included things such as details about the users' identities, their friend networks, what they had "liked" on their news feeds, and what pages

Christopher Wylie, *left*, is a former Cambridge Analytica employee. In 2018, he told US lawmakers that the company used Facebook to target people and trigger their racial biases.

they had "liked." That information could later be used to target users with specific digital ads.

One of the methods used on Facebook in 2014 to gain information about users and their friends was asking users to take a personality survey. To take the survey, users had to download an app first. That app gathered personal information not only from the user who downloaded it but also from friends on the user's network. Apps with this type of access to users' friends' data was previously allowed by Facebook, although Facebook has since banned the app and informed users whose information may have been shared through it. Facebook insists that Cambridge Analytica did not breach Facebook's security because it routinely allows access to user data for academic purposes. All Facebook users agree to the collection and possible use of their data when they create a Facebook account. Users also had to agree to the data harvesting when they downloaded the personality

"WE HAVE A RESPONSIBILITY TO PROTECT YOUR DATA, AND IF WE CAN'T THEN WE DON'T DESERVE TO SERVE YOU. I'VE BEEN WORKING TO UNDERSTAND EXACTLY WHAT HAPPENED AND HOW TO MAKE SURE THIS DOESN'T HAPPEN AGAIN."[10]

—MARK ZUCKERBERG ON CAMBRIDGE ANALYTICA'S ACCESS TO USER DATA, MARCH 21, 2018

survey app. Only about 270,000 people consented to it.[11] However, friends on their networks were also unknowingly giving up their data without having given their permission. In April 2018, Facebook noted that Cambridge Analytica could have got information on millions of Facebook users without the users' consent. The data collected was used to build software programs to predict and influence the voting choices of those users.

While Cambridge Analytica claims that it was collecting data within Facebook's guidelines, Facebook does have a policy that prohibits this kind of data from being sold or transferred "to any ad network, data broker or other advertising or monetization-related service."[12] That is exactly what Cambridge Analytica did in selling the data to the Trump campaign as part of its data

WORKING BEHIND THE SCENES

Cambridge Analytica has been accused of offering to entrap politicians. This means that the company would involve politicians in compromising situations that might damage their reputations as a way to discredit them. This could provide an advantage to those politicians' rivals. Alexander Nix is the former head of Cambridge Analytica. He reportedly told a potential client (who was actually a British television news reporter acting undercover) that his company could send an attractive woman to seduce a rival candidate and secretly videotape the encounter. He also suggested sending someone posing as a wealthy land developer to pass a bribe. Nix claimed that the company had "a long history of working behind the scenes."[13]

collection service. When Facebook learned that Cambridge Analytica had violated its terms of service, it removed the app from its site and demanded that the collected data be destroyed. It received certification from Cambridge Analytica that the data files had been destroyed, but it was a false certification. Facebook issued a statement in March 2018 that said in part, "Several days ago, we received reports that, contrary to the certifications we were given, not all data was deleted. We are moving aggressively to determine the accuracy of these claims. If true, this is another unacceptable violation of trust and the commitments they made."[14]

Facebook hired a digital forensics company to investigate Cambridge Analytica's activities. The company's investigations revealed that the Facebook data was still intact and available to anyone seeking to access it. The *New York Times* tested this by accessing and viewing these raw data files.

"I THINK THAT MAY BE WHAT THIS IS ALL ABOUT. YOUR RIGHT TO PRIVACY. THE LIMITS OF YOUR RIGHT TO PRIVACY. AND HOW MUCH YOU GIVE AWAY IN MODERN AMERICA IN THE NAME OF, QUOTE, CONNECTING PEOPLE AROUND THE WORLD."[15]

—SENATOR RICHARD J. DURBIN TO MARK ZUCKERBERG, APRIL 10, 2018

On May 2, 2018, Cambridge Analytica announced that it was filing for bankruptcy. This was a direct result of the Facebook data scandal and because of the intensive scrutiny Cambridge Analytica was undergoing regarding the 2016 election and Trump's campaign. In the statement issued by the company, it said that "the siege of media coverage has driven away virtually all of the Company's customers and suppliers. As a result, it has been determined that it is no longer viable to continue operating the business."[16] However, in early 2018, several of the executives from Cambridge Analytica joined a new company, called Emerdata.

MORE TO THE
STORY

ZUCKERBERG AND CONGRESS

As a result of Cambridge Analytica's use of Facebook data, as well as the revelation that Russian trolls had set up false accounts on the social media site and targeted voters with fake ads concerning the 2016 election and its candidates, Zuckerberg appeared before Congress in April 2018. He was there to answer questions about the site's security measures and the mishandling of its data.

Because of the discovery that Cambridge Analytica did use people's personal data accessed through Facebook, Facebook has been forced to reassess its security and how its users' data is being protected. Zuckerberg assured Congress that Facebook was using new artificial intelligence tools to detect any illegal or unacceptable activity on the site.

CHAPTER SIX

THE
INTERFERENCE

Following Trump's successful election in November 2016, people close to him began urging him to publicly address the issue of Russian hacking in the election. US intelligence agencies had already concluded that the interference was real. Trump's advisers urged him to bring the issue into the public eye. According to the *Washington Post*, Trump met with his advisers on January 6, 2017, in his Trump Tower headquarters in New York City.

During that meeting, the president-elect was urged to make a public statement about the intelligence agencies' finding. That way, he could put the matter behind him and it would give him the freedom to pursue a relationship with Putin once he was president.

Some people believe that Trump committed treason and that he and Russia worked together to sway the 2016 election.

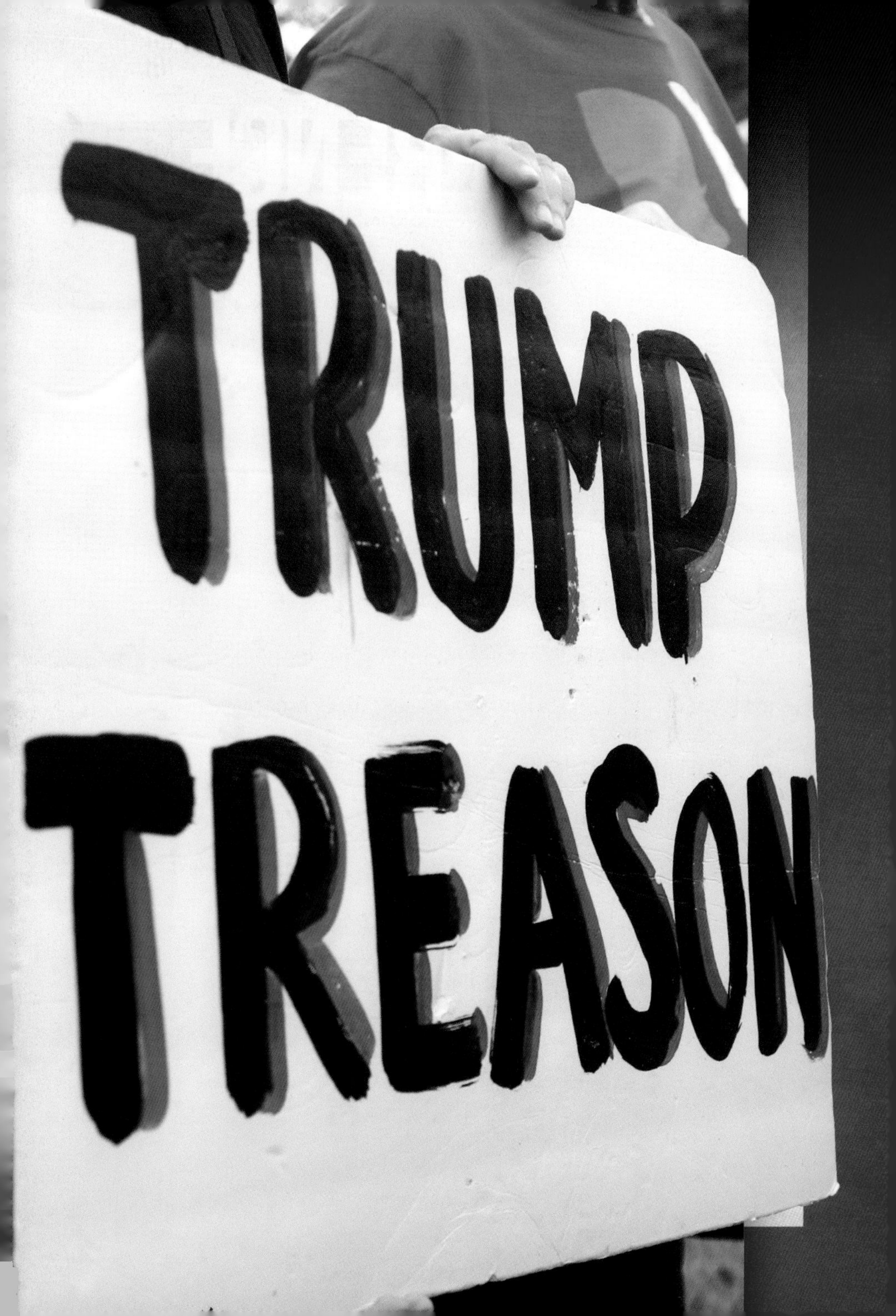
TRUMP
TREASON

AN INTELLIGENCE BOMBSHELL

The government had been aware of Russian interference in the 2016 election by August 2016, when President Obama and three of his top aides received a document from the CIA. It was marked as extremely sensitive information. The document detailed Putin's attempts to disrupt and discredit the 2016 presidential election through a cyber campaign. The report was based on intelligence received from within the Russian government. It revealed not only the plan to disrupt the election but also the intent to defeat Clinton and elect Trump.

Obama instructed his aides to assess the US election system and where there might be vulnerabilities, such as how voting was carried out. Homeland Security Secretary Jeh Johnson tried to make sure that the US voting systems were secure. But his plans were thwarted by some state officials who saw it as a federal takeover of state elections. At the same time, CIA director John Brennan contacted Alexander Bortnikov, the director of Russia's main security agency, and warned him about interfering in the US election.

The classified document, given to Obama and his aides, was kept under tight security until all the US intelligence agencies agreed with its findings. Then, a declassified version was released to the public in the last few weeks of the Obama administration.

The report forced Trump to meet with his closest advisers in order to plan what his official response should be. The report also caused Obama, in December 2016, to create a plan of sanctions and other means for punishing Russia and preventing it from interfering in US elections in the future. Sanctions included the expulsion of 35 Russian diplomats from the United States; the closing of two Russian compounds, which are groups of luxury homes shielded from the public and used by Russia diplomats; and some economic sanctions that were more symbolic

In 2017, John Brennan testified before lawmakers about the extent of Russia's actions in the 2016 election.

than punishing, such as no longer allowing Russian businesses to access some sources of loans and financing in the United States.[1]

TRUMP RESPONDS

Trump had already responded to the first reports of Russian meddling in December 2016, tweeting, "Unless you catch 'hackers' in the act, it is very hard to determine who was doing the hacking. Why wasn't this brought up before election?"[2] When told of the intelligence findings that uncovered Russian interference in the US election, President-elect Trump insisted that he won the elections entirely through his strategy, the message he gave to voters, and his personality and charisma, and not because of help from the Russians.

In June 2017, Putin claimed that perhaps the Russian cyberattacks were the work of "patriotic" Russians who might

"THE RUSSIANS HAD NO IMPACT ON OUR VOTES WHATSOEVER. BUT, CERTAINLY, THERE WAS MEDDLING AND PROBABLY THERE WAS MEDDLING FROM OTHER COUNTRIES AND MAYBE OTHER INDIVIDUALS. AND I THINK YOU HAVE TO BE REALLY WATCHING VERY CLOSELY. YOU DON'T WANT YOUR SYSTEM OF VOTES TO BE COMPROMISED IN ANY WAY. AND WE WON'T ALLOW THAT TO HAPPEN."[3]

—PRESIDENT DONALD TRUMP, MARCH 2018

be joining "the justified fight against those speaking ill of Russia."[4] But he denied the government's involvement. He added that the interference was never conducted on the government level.

SPEAR PHISHING?

Also in June 2017, the website the *Intercept* released an NSA report that detailed some of the hacking efforts on the US election that seemed to be linked to Russia. This included a cyberattack on at least one US supplier of voting machine software, VR Systems, as well as more than 100 spear phishing email attempts targeting local election officials.[5] It also cited the involvement of Russian intelligence members. According to the NSA report:

> *Russian General Staff Main Intelligence Directorate actors . . . executed cyber espionage operations against a named U.S. company in August 2016, evidently to obtain information on elections-related software and hardware solutions. . . . The actors likely used data obtained from that operation to . . . launch a voter registration-themed spear-phishing campaign targeting U.S. local government organizations.[6]*

The NSA report detailed the spear phishing attempts. Russian hackers sent emails to VR Systems, trying to trick employees into providing their user information and passwords. At least one account was compromised, and the Russian hackers used that information to start a separate phishing attack on more than 100 election officials.[7] If the recipients clicked on a link in the false email, the Russian hackers could then introduce a virus into the recipient's computer system. VR Systems sent emails to its customers advising them of the spear phishing attempts. It also said, "It is also important to note that none of our products perform the function of ballot marking, or tabulation of marked ballots."[8] In other words, while hackers could possibly infiltrate the software system through their hacking of employee emails, it only gave them access to voter information and not the ability to change any ballots or how they were counted.

DISTRIBUTING CLASSIFIED INFORMATION

At the same time as the hacking attempts on voting systems were revealed, the US Department of Justice announced that it was arresting a 25-year-old Georgia woman named Reality Leigh Winner. Winner worked for an intelligence agency contractor, and she was accused of printing out and mailing classified materials to a news outlet. Deputy Attorney General Rod Rosenstein said of the arrest, "People who are trusted with classified information and pledge to protect it must be held accountable when they violate that obligation."[9]

TIGHTENING SANCTIONS

On July 22, 2017, congressional leaders reached an expanded agreement concerning the sanctions that Obama had placed on Russia. The sanctions were to punish Russia for its election meddling as well as its aggression against its neighboring countries, such as Ukraine. The new legislation would also restrict Trump's ability to remove or modify the sanctions without Congress's approval. The White House claimed this would limit Trump's ability to adjust the sanctions in his diplomatic dealings with Russia. According to CNN, the Russian sanctions would target people and organizations that try to weaken US cybersecurity, do business with

In 2018, Trump spoke to Putin about Russia meddling in the election, and Putin denied that Russia interfered.

Russian defense and intelligence agencies, commit human rights abuses, or are involved in serious corruption.

The legislation also included 12 specific sanctions that could be used against Russia.[10] One sanction included freezing Russian bank accounts in the United States so that certain Russians could no longer access or use their money. Another involved revoking US visas that allow Russians to legally visit, live, and work in the United States.

Trump signed the sanctions bill on August 2, 2017—even though it limited his ability to modify those sanctions in the future—because it was overwhelmingly supported by the US House and Senate. In response to the sanctions placed on Russia by Congress in 2017, President Putin announced just a few days later that the United States had to remove 755 diplomatic employees from Russia.[11]

"THE BILL REMAINS SERIOUSLY FLAWED—PARTICULARLY BECAUSE IT ENCROACHES ON THE EXECUTIVE BRANCH'S AUTHORITY TO NEGOTIATE."[12]

—PRESIDENT DONALD TRUMP ON THE RUSSIAN SANCTIONS LEGISLATION, 2017

US secretary of the treasury Steven Mnuchin said US sanctions were intended to punish Russia for its actions across the globe.

CHAPTER SEVEN

MORE THAN
JUST POLITICS

O n March 15, 2018, the US Department of Homeland Security issued an alert entitled "Russian Government Cyber Activity Targeting Energy and Other Critical Infrastructure Sectors." The alert stated: "Since at least March 2016, Russian government cyber actors . . . targeted government entities and multiple U.S. critical infrastructure sectors, including the energy, nuclear, commercial facilities, water, aviation, and critical manufacturing sectors."[1]

The alert highlighted actions by cyber actors who were working for the Russian government. These actors targeted small commercial facilities with spear phishing and malware (malicious software designed to access, destroy, or disrupt computer systems). They eventually

Russian hackers accessed the computer networks of US energy facilities.

gained remote access to networks in the US energy sector. Often this access was gained through suppliers, who were trusted to provide goods and services to these targeted companies but often had less-secure internet networks. Once the cyber actors gained access, they were able to open and explore emails, files, and other materials. They collected information about the control system software that runs various energy systems.

NOTHING NEW

The official government announcement about the cyberattacks was released on the same day as the announcement of intelligence findings concerning Russian hacking and the 2016 election. The announcement came as no surprise to many experts. James Lewis, a cybersecurity expert and vice president of the Center for Strategic and International Studies, told National Public Radio, "The Russians have been doing this for years. The change is that the U.S. government came out and said the Russians hacked the utilities."[2]

However, the seriousness of the cyberattacks was not only that the Russians accessed the control systems of these plants but that they left behind ways for them to manipulate the control systems in the future. Joel Brenner, a former head of counterintelligence under the Obama administration, said, "They were placing the tools that they would have to place in order to turn off the power. That's a serious vulnerability for us, and we're not anywhere near ready to deal with it."[3] Russia had done the same thing in Ukraine in 2015, disrupting the power supply to more than 200,000 people.[4] US energy providers have studied the Ukraine attack to help them learn what happened and what measures might be taken in the event of a similar attack.

Disruption of the US power grid by cyberattacks could leave millions of Americans without power or water. It could also be expensive if the economy had to cope with the effects of those disabled services and bringing them back online. According to the London insurance company Lloyd's and

DOING THINGS THE OLD-FASHIONED WAY

While security and government officials are worried about possible Russian interference in the supply of energy to US customers, they do emphasize that the US power grid is protected by many different measures. One of them is simply retaining manual controls of power plant operations—not just digital, computerized controls. This enables plants to run without cyber elements that can be hacked.

> "THE REALITY IS THAT THE MODERN, DIGITAL, AND INTERCONNECTED WORLD CREATES THE CONDITIONS FOR SIGNIFICANT DAMAGE, AND WE KNOW THERE ARE HOSTILE ACTORS WITH THE SKILLS AND DESIRE TO CAUSE HARM."[6]
>
> **—TOM BOLT, DIRECTOR OF PERFORMANCE MANAGEMENT AT LLOYD'S**

the University of Cambridge's Centre for Risk Studies: "Experts predict [that the disruption of the power grid] would result in a rise in mortality rates as health and safety systems fail; a decline in trade as ports shut down; disruption to water supplies as electric pumps fail and chaos to transport networks as infrastructure collapses. The total impact to the US economy is estimated at $243 billion, rising to more than $1 trillion in the most extreme version of the scenario."[5]

THE AVIATION INDUSTRY

Russian cyber intrusions were not just limited to US power plants and the energy grid. In early 2017, the US aviation industry detected attacks on several US airlines or suppliers that produce aviation equipment. The intrusions were detected at the stage when hackers typically infiltrate a system just to perform surveillance, as well as test the defenses placed on the network. This helps hackers decide which software "weapons" could be used to attack the network. The 2017 attack had a limited effect on the aviation industry, but it did spark a more in-depth evaluation as to whether the aviation industry is safe from hacking.

Why is the aviation industry a target for Russian cyberattacks? Airlines have a huge effect on society, and if people aren't able to travel where they need to go and do so fairly easily, it affects the economy because regular business is difficult to carry out. In addition to disrupting business and reducing airline revenue, hacking could also make flying unsafe if hackers were able to control air traffic control programs.

"NOBODY WANTS A WAR. [THE HOSTILITIES TAKING PLACE NOW] ARE IN THE GRAY SPACE BETWEEN WAR AND PEACE."[7]

—JOEL BRENNER, ON RUSSIAN CYBER INTRUSIONS INTO US POWER PLANTS

"THOUSANDS OF TIMES A DAY"

Cyberattacks are not just an occasional occurrence. US energy secretary Rick Perry testified before a US House committee panel at the time of the US Department of Homeland Security report. He said the cyberattacks are "literally happening thousands of times a day." Perry noted that "the warfare that goes on in the cyberspace is real, it's serious."[8] He also said he didn't have confidence that the US government had enough strategies in place to deal with potential cyber threats.

There have also been incidents of Russian hackers accessing thousands of the Colorado Department of Transportation's computers—which were shut down after a malware attack—and cyberattacks on the Alyeska Pipeline Service Company. This company operates the trans-Alaska oil pipeline, which transports roughly 500,000 barrels of crude oil each day. The attack on

Rick Perry, *right*, participated in the Department of Homeland Security National Cybersecurity Summit in 2018. The summit worked at finding a way to protect US infrastructure.

Alyeska was unsuccessful, but as spokeswoman Kate Dugan said, "We know they are trying. The number grows every year."[9] Because the United States is heavily dependent on oil as a source of energy, it is particularly vulnerable to attacks on anything having to do with oil supplies and energy transportation. The entire electrical grid system, which is already overloaded and out of date, is vulnerable to hacking.

OFF THE GRID

One way that the United States could minimize the vulnerability of its power grid is by developing more sources of alternative and renewable energy, such as solar and wind. Many of these sources can operate as small grids that don't cover vast portions of the country as they do now. The grids could even specifically cover individual houses. Small grids reduce the risk of a large-scale cyberattack affecting millions of people. They also lessen the dependence on foreign oil sources and the vulnerabilities in the transportation of oil.

A BLIND EYE?

Despite the seriousness of the attacks on US infrastructure and the evidence that it is often perpetrated by hackers working for the Russian government, Trump has not taken a harder stand with Putin. On March 20, 2018, Trump called Putin to congratulate him on winning reelection in Russia. Most of the world considered the Russian election to be a sham as one of the opposition figures, Alexei Navalny,

News agencies in Russia caught some people voting multiple times in the Russian election.

was barred from the race. There were also reports of voting irregularities, such as ballots already being in ballot boxes before the election began and actions taken to bar observation of the election by outsiders. Trump told CNN, "I had a call with President Putin and congratulated him on the victory. . . . The call had to do also with the fact that we will probably get together in the not too distant future."[10]

Trump's call was criticized by many government leaders, such as Arizona senator John McCain, who tweeted: "An American president does not lead the Free World by congratulating dictators on winning sham elections. And by doing so with Vladimir Putin, President

Trump insulted every Russian citizen who was denied the right to vote in a free and fair election."[11] Trump's own advisers had told him before the call that he should not congratulate Putin. They added that Trump should make some sort of statement to President Putin concerning the Russian cyberattacks and interference in the 2016 election. Trump's indication that he and Putin might meet soon was also a security concern to US government officials.

Trump's relationship with Putin seemed to be uneven. On one hand, Trump signed the bill imposing sanctions on Russia. But on the other hand, he seemed to be maintaining a friendly relationship and turning a blind eye to Russia's own election irregularities and its possible meddling in other countries' elections. It was Trump's relationship with Russia and Putin, as well as Trump's family and his business dealings, that would become a major focus of the next step: the Special Counsel investigation by Robert Mueller.

FROM THE HEADLINES

THE TRUMP AND PUTIN SUMMIT

In July 2018, Trump and Putin met in Helsinki, Finland. Just days before the meeting, 12 Russians were charged by the US Department of Justice for using malicious software and spear phishing emails to interfere in the 2016 election.[12] However, during the meeting, Trump failed to hold Putin responsible for Russia's actions during the election. Trump disregarded US intelligence reports and publicly took Putin's side on the issue. During a joint press conference with Putin after their meeting, Trump said, "I have great confidence in my intelligence people, but I will tell you that President Putin was extremely strong and powerful in his denial today."[13]

Politicians from both sides of the political aisle condemned Trump's words. Republican US representative Paul Ryan said, "There is no question that Russia interfered in our elections. . . . The President must appreciate that Russia is not our ally. There is no moral equivalence between the United States and Russia, which remains hostile to our most basic values and ideals."[14]

Before the joint press conference in Helsinki, Trump and Putin had a two-hour private meeting.

US Democratic senator Chuck Schumer said, "For the president of the United States to side with President Putin against American law enforcement, American defense officials, and American intelligence agencies is thoughtless, dangerous and weak. The president is putting himself over our country."[15] After receiving this harsh feedback, Trump said that he had misspoken at the joint press conference and said US intelligence agencies have his "full faith and support."[16]

CHAPTER EIGHT

THE MUELLER
INVESTIGATION

The investigations into Russian hacking related to the 2016 US presidential election were complicated by the fact that, unlike previous presidents, Trump had already had business and personal relationships with Russia. Trump's ties with Russia go much further back than his political career. In 1987, he visited what was then the Soviet Union. He told reporters there that he was exploring the idea of building a Trump Tower hotel in Moscow near the Kremlin, and possibly another in Leningrad, now Saint Petersburg. However, the hotels were never built. Trump also explored other possible deals, trademarks, and sponsorships in the country. These included staging events such as a Soviet boxing match that would take

Beginning in 2017, Robert Mueller started investigating any possible connections between Trump's campaign and Russia.

place in the United States and commissioning a giant statue of Christopher Columbus to be made by a Russian artist and put up in New York City.

Trump also met with several Soviet and Russian leaders over time, including Soviet Union leader Mikhail Gorbachev and Russian president Boris Yeltsin. Trump developed real estate in Florida, and the properties became a haven for rich Russians to visit. There were other real estate deals between Trump and Russians, as well as attempts to start a Trump reality show in Russia and to market Trump brand alcohol there.

Between 1996 and 2015, Trump was one owner of the Miss Universe Organization. This organization runs pageant events. As early as 2013, Trump reached out to Putin just before Trump hosted a Miss Universe pageant in Moscow—an event Trump produced and which made him a great deal of money. Following the 2013 pageant, Trump said of Putin: "I do have a relationship [with Putin] . . . and I can tell you that he's very interested in what we're doing here today. He's probably very interested

"DO YOU THINK PUTIN WILL BE GOING TO THE MISS UNIVERSE PAGEANT IN NOVEMBER IN MOSCOW—IF SO, WILL HE BECOME MY BEST FRIEND?"[1]

—DONALD TRUMP, 2013

in what you and I are saying today and I'm sure he's going to be seeing it in some form. But I do have a relationship with him."[2]

The web of relationships, both political and business oriented, between Trump and Russia would become more complex and interwoven through the 2016 election. Following the election and Trump's win, Russian advisers and diplomats worked to create ways to communicate with Trump outside of normal diplomatic methods.

ROBERT MUELLER APPOINTED

The complicated web of relationships surrounding Trump and Russia were concerning to many people. Adding fuel to the fire, Trump suddenly fired FBI director James Comey on May 9, 2017. At the time of his dismissal, Comey was investigating whether Trump's campaign had colluded with Russia during the election. Trump presented various reasons as to why he fired Comey. At one point, Trump said, "I was going to fire Comey. . . . When I decided to just do it, I said to myself—I said, you know, this Russia thing with Trump and Russia is a made-up story." Trump also said he fired Comey because "he's the wrong man for that position."[3]

A little more than one week after Comey was fired, a formal investigation of the election and any other Russian interference was undertaken by the US Department of Justice. On May 17, 2017, Deputy Attorney General Rod Rosenstein, the second-highest official in the US Department of Justice, appointed former FBI director Robert Mueller as Special Counsel, which is the title that the Department of Justice assigns its investigators. Mueller's job was to investigate possible collusion between the Trump campaign and Russia.

Trump and Comey spoke many times before Comey's sudden dismissal from the FBI.

Mueller had been the FBI director for 12 years, beginning with President George W. Bush and continuing under Obama. He had a good reputation and was considered to be nonpartisan, meaning that he was not loyal to one political party more than the other. Rosenstein's order for a special investigation allowed Mueller to look into the Russian government's efforts to interfere with the 2016 election, links or cooperative actions between Russia and the Trump campaign, and any other matters that might arise from the investigation. This last point could possibly allow Mueller to investigate President Trump himself if Mueller felt it was warranted.

Mueller had the power to hire federal prosecutors who could assist with the investigation and research process, and he hired 17 of them.[4] The prosecutors had

WHAT CAN A SPECIAL COUNSEL DO?

A special counsel conducting an investigation has the same powers as a US attorney. He or she can officially request records, bring criminal charges, and prosecute anyone who interferes with the investigation through crimes such as perjury, obstruction of justice, destruction of evidence, and intimidation of witnesses. A special counsel can request that the US Department of Justice widen his or her jurisdiction as well. The counselor does not have a day-to-day boss, but the attorney general can request an explanation for any of the counselor's actions and decide whether those actions can continue.

expertise in areas such as money laundering, fraud, foreign bribery, and organized crime. Mueller could not be fired by anyone other than Deputy Attorney General Rosenstein. Usually, a special counsel can only be fired by the attorney general. However, Attorney General Jeff Sessions removed himself from the investigation. Sessions removed himself because he had previously acted as an adviser for the Trump campaign, and he would have had a conflict of interest. But if the president decided to, he could replace the deputy attorney general at any time.

GETTING STARTED

On July 26, 2017, federal agents raided Paul Manafort's home. By October, Manafort and his business partner Rick Gates were accused of money laundering and other charges. Many of the charges were related to Russia and Ukraine, including dealings with Russian oligarchs. Manafort initially pleaded not guilty. However, in August 2018, a jury found Manafort guilty of charges relating to bank fraud, tax fraud, and a failure to disclose foreign bank accounts. Although Manafort's conviction isn't related to collusion with Russia, "having one's former campaign chair

Paul Manafort's trial began on July 31, 2018.

end up as a convicted felon is not good news," reporter

Anthony Zurcher says.[5] In September 2018, Manafort

pleaded guilty to conspiring against the United States. He

agreed to work with federal officials as they continued

their investigation. Gates eventually pleaded guilty to

lesser charges.

Trump's national security adviser, Michael Flynn,

admitted to having a series of phone conversations with

Sergey Kislyak, the Russian ambassador to the United

States. Some of these conversations took place on

nonsecure channels and involved political matters such

as possible sanctions by the United States against Russia.

Flynn resigned in February 2017. He pleaded guilty to lying to the FBI about his contacts with Russia.

George Papadopoulos was a foreign policy adviser to Trump's campaign. He made news headlines regarding emails during the 2016 campaign. While drinking in a London bar one night in May 2016, he told Australia's top diplomat in Britain, Alexander Downer, that Russia had incriminating emails about Clinton. These were reportedly thousands of stolen emails that could embarrass Clinton and harm her campaign. When the leaked emails began appearing online, the Australian government told its American counterparts about the incident. Papadopoulos lied to the FBI about his Russian contacts. He pleaded guilty and agreed to cooperate with Mueller's investigation.

On February 16, 2018, Mueller charged 13 Russians and three Russian companies with conspiracy to interfere

"HE NEVER SHOWED UP AT TRUMP TOWER. NEVER HAD ANY INTERACTION WITH ANY OF THE CAMPAIGN LEADERS AROUND ME, AND THE LEADERS OF THE WASHINGTON OFFICE OF THE CAMPAIGN DIDN'T EVEN KNOW WHO HE WAS UNTIL HIS NAME APPEARED IN THE PRESS. . . . HE WAS THE COFFEE BOY."[6]

—MICHAEL CAPUTO, A FORMER TRUMP CAMPAIGN ADVISER, SPEAKING ABOUT PAPADOPOULOS'S ROLE IN THE TRUMP CAMPAIGN, OCTOBER 31, 2017

with the 2016 US presidential election.[7] One company

charged was the IRA, based in Saint Petersburg, Russia,

which had created the fake Facebook troll accounts.

On April 3, 2018, Mueller charged a Dutch attorney,

Alex van der Zwaan, with lying and deleting emails that

had been requested by Mueller's investigation team.

Van der Zwaan is the son of a prominent lawyer based in

Russia, and he lied to the FBI about his contacts in Russia.

The attorney also had ties to Gates and Manafort. Van der

Zwaan had apparently communicated with both Gates

and someone with ties to Russian intelligence. Van der

Zwaan lied to investigators when he was interviewed. He

was sentenced by a federal judge to 30 days in jail and a

$20,000 fine when he admitted to lying.[8]

Michael Cohen is another former Trump associate who

has become instrumental in the Mueller investigation on

Russian interference. Cohen was Trump's former personal

lawyer. Cohen came under investigation for campaign

finance violations and bank fraud. His offices were raided

by officials from the Mueller investigation. This April 2018

raid found audio recordings and other material relating to

Trump and his campaign and personal dealings.

FROM THE
HEADLINES

SPIES AND POISON

On March 4, 2018, former Russian spy Sergei Skripal, age 66, and his daughter Yulia, age 33, were found unconscious on a park bench in Salisbury, England. They had both been poisoned with a nerve agent, which is a chemical that disrupts the communication between the body's nerves and organs. Both survived the encounter. This particular nerve agent was known to be manufactured by Russia. Several police officers who responded were also affected.

Skripal was a former Russian military officer who acted as a double agent for the United Kingdom's intelligence services, becoming a British spy. The poisoning was believed to be the work of Russian intelligence agencies. Immediately following the incident, British prime minister Theresa May said, "Either this was a direct act by the Russian state against our country, or the Russian government lost control of this potentially catastrophically damaging nerve agent and allowed it to get into the hands of others."[9] The United States and the European Union also supported

First responders to the Salisbury poisoning wore chemical suits to protect themselves from the nerve agent.

May in holding Russia accountable. Russia claimed that the incident was staged, perhaps by the British themselves, to turn public opinion against Putin, as well as a fabrication of the US and British governments. As a result of the incident, the United Kingdom expelled 23 Russian diplomats.[10] Other countries, including the United States, did the same. Later in 2018, another couple in Amesbury, England, was poisoned by the same nerve agent, and one of them died. Officials believed the nerve agent may have been left over from the first incident in March.

Michael Cohen expressed willingness to cooperate with federal investigators after the raid on his offices.

Cohen may have a great deal of information to provide investigators about Trump's business dealings and any Russian election collusion. In July 2018, Cohen claimed that Trump was aware of the 2016 meeting between Russians and his campaign staff, where the Russians promised information on Clinton. Trump has denied any knowledge about this meeting. And although lying to the public isn't a crime, Trump could face legal troubles in Mueller's cases regarding attempts to obstruct the investigation and conspire with Russia in the election.

THE FUTURE OF RUSSIA AND US ELECTIONS

The investigation into the degree of Russian interference in the 2016 election carries with it another question: What will happen during the 2020 election, especially if Trump is running for reelection? Most political analysts feel that further Russian interference is a given, not just a possibility.

One former US government official spoke anonymously with *Vanity Fair* reporter Nick Bilton in June 2018. Concerning Trump losing the presidency, the official said, "Russia is going to do everything it can to ensure that doesn't happen. They'll hack the voting booths, if they haven't already; they'll quadruple their efforts on social media; they'll do things we haven't even thought of yet."[11]

Many of Russia's tactics in 2016, such as using social media and digital platforms to infiltrate and manipulate US politics, will most likely be refined and made even more powerful for the 2020 elections. Indeed, Russian hackers were already at work before the 2018 US midterm elections. In August 2018, software company Microsoft said it had discovered that Russian hackers attempted to steal data from political groups. In addition, around this time, Twitter and Facebook took down hundreds of groups, pages, and accounts that were linked to Russia. Facebook noted that it removed these because they "can be linked to sources the US government has previously identified as Russian military intelligence services."[12]

Political experts see that Russia can only gain if it is able to pit the United States against itself. By creating mistrust and divisions, Russia can make the rest of the world wonder about the legitimacy of the US government.

THE INVESTIGATION CONTINUES

As of September 2018, the special investigation into Russia's dealings with the US presidential election and other issues continued. Many political observers believed that Mueller would eventually subpoena Trump, although it is unclear whether a sitting president can legally be subpoenaed to testify. A subpoena is an order for a person to appear in court. It is likely that only the Supreme Court could make that decision. The Trump Organization was already subpoenaed in March 2018, when it was forced to turn over certain documents relating to Russia and Trump's businesses.

Trump has complained that the Mueller investigation is interfering with his ability to conduct his presidential duties. The White House has stated that Trump is cooperating fully with the investigation, but Trump tweeted on May 2, 2018, "There was no Collusion (it is a Hoax) and there is no Obstruction of Justice (that is a setup & trap)."[14] Obstruction of justice is the act of willfully and deliberately interfering with the process of a law investigation.

As of mid-2018, there were many questions that have not yet been answered surrounding what might happen with the special investigation. These questions included whether Mueller could be fired by Trump, or whether Mueller could lose his position as special counsel if Rosenstein were replaced. Americans watched the investigation closely to see what conclusions it would reach, and US intelligence agencies were on guard for future hacking and meddling in American elections.

ESSENTIAL
FACTS

MAJOR EVENTS

- In 2014, the data harvesting company Cambridge Analytica began using Facebook accounts to access user data.

- From June 2015 to May 2017, Russian trolls bought ads on Facebook to influence voters.

- In September 2015, emails from the Democratic National Committee were hacked and released to the public.

- In November 2016, Donald Trump won the presidential election, defeating Hillary Clinton.

- In May 2017, the US Department of Justice opened a special investigation, headed by Robert Mueller, into the Russian hacking situation.

- On February 16, 2018, Mueller charged 13 Russians and three Russian companies with conspiracy to interfere with the 2016 US election.

KEY PLAYERS

- Donald Trump's connections to Russia led some people to suspect that his campaign worked with Russia to get him elected as president.

- Vladimir Putin has consistently denied any involvement by the Russian government in the 2016 US presidential election.

- Robert Mueller headed the investigation into Russia's involvement in the 2016 US presidential election and searched for any collusion between Russia and the Trump campaign.

IMPACT ON SOCIETY

Incidents of Russian hacking have made Americans aware that US elections aren't safe from foreign interference. The hacking has also made people aware that their feelings toward political candidates can be manipulated by social media run by Russian trolls. Russia's actions have also caused people to question if there may have been collusion between the Trump campaign and Russia.

QUOTE

"Based on briefings we have received, we have concluded that the Russian intelligence agencies are making a serious and concerted effort to influence the U.S. election."

—Dianne Feinstein and Adam Schiff, members of the House and Senate Intelligence Committees, 2016

GLOSSARY

ADVERSARY
Someone's opponent in a dispute or conflict.

ARSENAL
A supply of weapons.

CAPITALIST
Having to do with an economic system in which businesses are privately owned and operated for the purpose of making a profit.

COLLUDE
To secretly work together with the intent of cheating someone or something.

CYBERATTACK
An attempt to damage or destroy a computer network or system.

CYBERESPIONAGE

The act of using a computer network to obtain illegal access to secret information.

DEMOGRAPHIC

A particular group within the population, defined by factors such as race, age, income, or education.

HACKER

A person who uses computers to gain unauthorized access to another computer in order to view, copy, or destroy data.

MONEY LAUNDERING

Hiding the true source of income from criminal activity by using a front, such as an actual business.

SANCTION

An action taken to punish a country or force it to follow international laws.

TIME STAMP

A digital record documenting when an event happened.

ADDITIONAL
RESOURCES

SELECTED BIBLIOGRAPHY

"Cold War History." *History*, n.d., history.com. Accessed 28 June 2018.

Fessler, Pam. "Report: Russia Launched Cyberattack on Voting Vendor ahead of Election." *NPR*, 5 June 2017, npr.org. Accessed 28 June 2018.

Krieg, Gregory. "The Day That Changed Everything: Election 2016, As It Happened." *CNN*, 8 Nov. 2017, cnn.com. Accessed 28 June 2018.

FURTHER READINGS

Higgins, Melissa. *Cybersecurity*. Abdo, 2016.

Streissguth, Tom. *The 2016 Presidential Election*. Abdo, 2018.

ONLINE RESOURCES

Booklinks
NONFICTION NETWORK
FREE! ONLINE NONFICTION RESOURCES

To learn more about Russian hacking in American elections, visit **abdobooklinks.com**. These links are routinely monitored and updated to provide the most current information available.

MORE INFORMATION

For more information on this subject, contact or visit the following organizations:

FairVote
6930 Carroll Avenue, Suite 240
Takoma Park, MD 20912
301-270-4616
fairvote.org
FairVote is an organization that works for nonpartisan election reforms that make sure that Americans have a working representational democracy, more choices, and a strong voice.

US Department of Justice
950 Pennsylvania Avenue NW
Washington, DC 20530-0001
202-353-1555
justice.gov
The US Department of Justice works to protect the United States from domestic and foreign threats, uphold the law, and punish people who break the law.

SOURCE
NOTES

CHAPTER 1. ELECTION DAY 2016

1. Gregory Krieg. "The Day That Changed Everything: Election 2016, As It Happened." *CNN*, 8 Nov. 2017, edition.cnn.com. Accessed 27 Aug. 2018.

2. Krieg, "The Day That Changed Everything."

3. Krieg, "The Day That Changed Everything."

4. "Hillary Clinton's Concession Speech (Full Text)." *CNN*, 9 Nov. 2016, cnn.com. Accessed 27 Aug. 2018.

5. Cynthia McFadden et al. "U.S. Intel: Russia Compromised Seven States Prior to 2016 Election." *NBC News*, 28 Feb. 2018, nbcnews.com. Accessed 27 Aug. 2018.

6. David Jackson. "Donald Trump Accepts GOP Nomination, Says 'I Alone Can Fix' System." *USA Today*, 21 July 2016, usatoday.com. Accessed 27 Aug. 2018.

7. Michael Isikoff. *Russian Roulette: The Inside Story of Putin's War on America and the Election of Donald Trump.* Twelve, 2018. 276.

8. Jill Dougherty. "Clinton 'Reset Button' Gift to Russian FM Gets Lost in Translation." *CNN*, 6 Mar. 2009, politicalticker.blogs.cnn.com. Accessed 27 Aug. 2018.

9. Isikoff, *Russian Roulette*, 278.

10. Isikoff, *Russian Roulette*, 277.

CHAPTER 2. A COLD WAR LEGACY

1. Andrew Glass. "Bernard Baruch Coins Term 'Cold War,' April 16, 1947." *Politico*, 16 Apr. 2010, politico.com. Accessed 27 Aug. 2018.

2. "Space Program." *John F. Kennedy Presidential Library and Museum*, n.d., jfklibrary.org. Accessed 27 Aug. 2018.

CHAPTER 3. HACKING AN ELECTION

1. Eric Lipton et al. "The Perfect Weapon: How Russian Cyberpower Invaded the U.S." *New York Times*, 13 Dec. 2016, nytimes.com. Accessed 27 Aug. 2018.

2. Eric Lipton. "How We Identified the D.N.C. Hack's 'Patient Zero.'" *New York Times*, 20 Dec. 2016, nytimes.com. Accessed 27 Aug. 2018.

3. Jim Sciutto. "How One Typo Helped Let Russian Hackers In." *CNN*, 27 June 2017, cnn.com. Accessed 27 Aug. 2018.

4. Daniel Strauss. "Podesta: 'I'm Not Happy about Being Hacked by the Russians.'" Politico, 7 Oct. 2016, politico.com. Accessed 27 Aug. 2018.

5. Sciutto, "How One Typo Helped Let Russian Hackers In."

6. Sciutto, "How One Typo Helped Let Russian Hackers In."

7. "What Is WikiLeaks." *WikiLeaks*, 3 Nov. 2015, wikileaks.org. Accessed 27 Aug. 2018.

8. Ashley Parker and David E. Sanger. "Donald Trump Calls on Russia to Find Hillary Clinton's Missing Emails." *New York Times*, 27 July 2016, nytimes.com. Accessed 27 Aug. 2018.

9. John Micklethwait. "Vladimir Putin Just Wants to Be Friends." *Bloomberg Businessweek*, 8 Sept. 2016, bloomberg.com. Accessed 27 Aug. 2018.

CHAPTER 4. A TANGLED WEB

1. "Feinstein, Schiff Statement on Russian Hacking." *United States Senator for California Dianne Feinstein*, 22 Sept. 2016, feinstein.senate.gov. Accessed 27 Aug. 2018.

2. "Feinstein, Schiff Statement on Russian Hacking."

3. "Read the Emails on Donald Trump Jr.'s Russia Meeting." *New York Times*, 11 July 2017, nytimes.com. Accessed 27 Aug. 2018.

4. "Manafort Had $10 Million Loan from Russian Oligarch: Court Filing." *Reuters*, 27 June 2018, reuters.com. Accessed 27 Aug. 2018.

5. Tom Winter and Ken Dilanian. "Donald Trump Aide Paul Manafort Scrutinized for Russian Business Ties." *NBC News*, 18 Aug 2016, nbcnews.com. Accessed 27 Aug. 2018.

6. "Presidential Results." *CNN*, 9 Nov. 2016, cnn.com. Accessed 27 Aug. 2018.

7. "Background to 'Assessing Russian Activities and Intentions in Recent US Elections': The Analytic Process and Cyber Incident Attribution." *Office of the Director of National Intelligence*, 6 Jan. 2017, dni.gov. Accessed 27 Aug. 2018.

CHAPTER 5. TROLLING ON FACEBOOK

1. Monica Anderson. "Social Media Causes Some Users to Rethink Their Views on an Issue." *Pew Research Center*, 7 Nov. 2016, pewresearch.org. Accessed 27 Aug. 2018.

2. "Our Mission." *Facebook Newsroom*, n.d., newsroom.fb.com. Accessed 27 Aug. 2018.

3. Selena Larson. "Mark Zuckerberg: The Idea That Fake News Influenced the Election Is 'Crazy.'" *CNN*, 10 Nov. 2016, money.cnn.com. Accessed 27 Aug. 2018.

4. Scott Shane and Vindu Goel. "Fake Russian Facebook Accounts Bought $100,000 in Political Ads." *New York Times*, 6 Sept. 2017, nytimes.com. Accessed 27 Aug. 2018.

5. Shane and Goel, "Fake Russian Facebook Accounts."

6. Jason Murdock. "What Is the Internet Research Agency? Facebook Shuts Hundreds of Accounts Linked to Russian Troll Factory." *Newsweek*, 4 Apr. 2018, newsweek.com. Accessed 27 Aug. 2018.

7. Murdock, "What Is the Internet Research Agency?"

8. Manu Raju et al. "Exclusive: Russian-Linked Facebook Ads Targeted Michigan and Wisconsin." *CNN*, 4 Oct. 2017, cnn.com. Accessed 27 Aug. 2018.

9. Paul Lewis et al. "Cambridge Analytica Academic's Work Upset University Colleagues." *Guardian*, 24 Mar. 2018, theguardian.com. Accessed 27 Aug. 2018.

10. Jeremy B. White. "Mark Zuckerberg Speaks on Cambridge Analytica Data Controversy: 'We Made Mistakes.'" *Independent*, 21 Mar. 2018, independent.co.uk. Accessed 27 Aug. 2018.

11. Kevin Granville. "Facebook and Cambridge Analytica: What You Need to Know as Fallout Widens." *New York Times*, 19 Mar. 2018, nytimes.com. Accessed 27 Aug. 2018.

12. "Facebook Platform Policy." *Facebook*, n.d., developers.facebook.com. Accessed 27 Aug. 2018.

13. Matthew Rosenberg. "Cambridge Analytica, Trump-Tied Political Firm, Offered to Entrap Politicians." *New York Times*, 19 Mar. 2018, nytimes.com. Accessed 27 Aug. 2018.

14. Paul Grewal. "Suspending Cambridge Analytica and SCL Group from Facebook." *Facebook Newsroom*, 16 Mar. 2018, newsroom.fb.com. Accessed 27 Aug. 2018.

15. "Mark Zuckerberg Testimony: Senators Question Facebook's Commitment to Privacy." *New York Times*, 10 Apr. 2018, nytimes.com. Accessed 27 Aug. 2018.

SOURCE NOTES
CONTINUED

16. "Cambridge Analytica and SCL Elections Commence Insolvency Proceedings and Release Results of Independent Investigation into Recent Allegations." *CA Commercial*, 2 May 2018, ca-commercial.com. Accessed 27 Aug. 2018.

CHAPTER 6. THE INTERFERENCE

1. Greg Miller et al. "Obama's Secret Struggle to Punish Russia for Putin's Election Assault." *Washington Post*, 23 June 2017, washingtonpost.com. Accessed 27 Aug. 2018.

2. Kaveh Waddell. "Trump Is Wrong That Investigators Have to Catch Hackers in the Act." *Atlantic*, 12 Dec. 2016, theatlantic.com. Accessed 27 Aug. 2018.

3. "Remarks by President Trump and Prime Minister Löfven of Sweden in Joint Press Conference." *White House*, 6 Mar. 2016, whitehouse.gov. Accessed 27 Aug. 2018.

4. "Putin: Patriotic Russians May Be Involved in Hacking." *BBC*, 1 June 2017, bbc.com. Accessed 27 Aug. 2018.

5. Matthew Cole et al. "Top-Secret NSA Report Details Russian Hacking Effort Days before 2016 Election." *Intercept*, 5 June 2017, theintercept.com. Accessed 27 Aug. 2018.

6. Cole et al. "Top-Secret NSA Report Details Russian Hacking."

7. Pam Fessler. "Report: Russia Launched Cyberattack on Voting Vendor ahead of Election." *NPR*, 5 June 2017, npr.org. Accessed 27 Aug. 2018.

8. Fessler, "Report: Russia Launched Cyberattack on Voting Vendor ahead of Election."

9. "Federal Government Contractor in Georgia Charged with Removing and Mailing Classified Materials to a News Outlet." *United States Department of Justice*, 5 June 2017, justice.gov. Accessed 27 Aug. 2018.

10. Angela Dewan. "Russia Sanctions: What You Need to Know." *CNN*, 2 Aug. 2017, cnn.com. Accessed 27 Aug. 2018.

11. Neil MacFarquhar. "Putin, Responding to Sanctions, Orders U.S. to Cut Diplomatic Staff by 755." *New York Times*, 30 July 2017, nytimes.com. Accessed 27 Aug. 2018.

12. "Statement by President Donald J. Trump on Signing the 'Countering America's Adversaries through Sanctions Act.'" *White House*, 2 Aug. 2017, whitehouse.gov. Accessed 27 Aug. 2018.

CHAPTER 7. MORE THAN JUST POLITICS

1. "Russian Government Cyber Activity Targeting Energy and Other Critical Infrastructure Sectors." *US Department of Homeland Security*, 15 Mar. 2018, us-cert.gov. Accessed 27 Aug. 2018.

2. Brian Naylor. "Russia Hacked U.S. Power Grid—So What Will the Trump Administration Do about It?" *NPR*, 23 Mar. 2018, npr.org. Accessed 27 Aug. 2018.

3. Naylor, "Russia Hacked U.S. Power Grid."

4. Patrick Tucker. "The Ukrainian Blackout and the Future of War." *Defense One*, 9 Mar. 2016, defenseone.com. Accessed 27 Aug. 2018.

5. "New Lloyd's Study Highlights Wide Ranging Implications of Cyber Attacks." *Lloyd's*, 8 July 2015, lloyds.com. Accessed 27 Aug. 2018.

6. "New Lloyd's Study Highlights Wide Ranging Implications of Cyber Attacks."

7. Naylor, "Russia Hacked U.S. Power Grid."

8. Jason Le Miere. "Russian Hackers Attacked U.S. Nuclear, Aviation and Power Grid Infrastructure, FBI and DHS Warn." *Newsweek*, 15 Mar. 2018, newsweek.com. Accessed 27 Aug. 2018.

9. Ari Natter. "Threat from Cyber Hackers Is Growing, U.S. Grid Regulator Says." *Bloomberg*, 23 Mar. 2016, bloomberg.com. Accessed 27 Aug. 2018.

10. Dan Merica. "Trump Congratulates Putin on Winning Reelection, Gets Slammed by McCain." *CNN*, 21 Mar. 2018, cnn.com. Accessed 27 Aug. 2018.

11. Merica, "Trump Congratulates Putin."

12. "Twelve Russians Charged with US 2016 Election Hack." *BBC*, 13 July 2016, bbc.com. Accessed 27 Aug. 2018.

13. Jeremy Diamond. "Trump Sides with Putin over US Intelligence." *CNN*, 16 July 2018, cnn.com. Accessed 27 Aug. 2018.

14. Diamond, "Trump Sides with Putin over US Intelligence."

15. Lauren Gambino. "Trump's Surrender to Putin Greeted with Outrage by Democrats and Republicans." *Guardian*, 16 July 2018, theguardian.com. Accessed 27 Aug. 2018.

16. "Trump Putin: US President Reverses Remarks on Russia Meddling." *BBC*, 18 July 2018, bbc.com. Accessed 27 Aug. 2018.

CHAPTER 8. THE MUELLER INVESTIGATION

1. Abbie VanSickle. "Confused by Trump's Russia Ties? This Timeline Breaks It Down for You." *Medium*, 21 Mar. 2017, medium.com. Accessed 27 Aug. 2018.

2. VanSickle, "Confused by Trump's Russia Ties?"

3. Linda Qiu. "Did Trump Fire Comey over the Russia Inquiry or Not?" *New York Times*, 31 May 2018, nytimes.com. Accessed 27 Aug. 2018.

4. "Special Counsel: What Is It and What Is Robert Mueller Doing?" *BBC*, 20 Feb. 2018, bbc.com. Accessed 27 Aug. 2018.

5. Anthony Zurcher. "Will Donald Trump Remain Bulletproof after Manafort and Cohen?" *BBC*, 22 Aug. 2018, bbc.com. Accessed 27 Aug. 2018.

6. Maegan Vazquez. "Ex-Trump Campaign Adviser: Papadopoulos Was Just a 'Coffee Boy.'" *CNN*, 31 Oct. 2017, cnn.com. Accessed 27 Aug. 2018.

7. "Timeline of Mueller Probe of Trump Campaign and Russia." *Reuters*, 10 Apr. 2018, reuters.com. Accessed 27 Aug. 2018.

8. Katelyn Polantz and Liz Stark. "Dutch Lawyer Is First Person to be Sentenced in Mueller Probe, Gets 30 Days in Prison." *CNN*, 3 Apr. 2018, cnn.com. Accessed 27 Aug. 2018.

9. Holly Ellyatt. "Russia Has No Connection to Ex-Spy Nerve Agent Attack, Foreign Minister Says." *CNBC*, 13 Mar. 2018, cnbc.com. Accessed 27 Aug. 2018.

10. "Western Countries Expel Some 100 Russian Diplomats over Skripal Case." *Sputnik International*, 27 Mar. 2018, sputniknews.com. Accessed 27 Aug. 2018.

11. Nick Bilton. "'The Russians Play Hard': Inside Russia's Attempt to Hack 2018—and 2020." *Vanity Fair*, 22 June 2018, vanityfair.com. Accessed 27 Aug. 2018.

12. "Microsoft Blocks Russian Hack, as Facebook and Twitter Remove Hundreds of Accounts." *ABC News*, 21 Aug. 2018, abc.net.au. Accessed 27 Aug. 2018.

13. "Key Quotes from Congress' Hearing on Russia and the U.S. Election." *Reuters*, 20 Mar. 2017, reuters.com. Accessed 27 Aug. 2018.

14. David Jackson. "Donald Trump Claims Robert Mueller Probe Is Interfering with His Presidential Duties." *USA Today*, 2 May 2018, usatoday.com. Accessed 27 Aug. 2018.

INDEX

ABOUT THE
AUTHORS

DUCHESS HARRIS, JD, PHD

Professor Harris is the chair of the American Studies department at Macalester College and curator of the Duchess Harris Collection of ABDO books. She is the author and coauthor of recently released ABDO books including *Hidden Human Computers: The Black Women of NASA*, *Black Lives Matter*, and *Race and Policing*.

Before working with ABDO, she authored several other books on the topics of race, culture, and American history. She served as an associate editor for *Litigation News*, the American Bar Association Section of Litigation's quarterly flagship publication, and was the first editor in chief of *Law Raza*, an interactive online journal covering race and the law, published at William Mitchell College of Law. She has earned a PhD in American Studies from the University of Minnesota and a JD from William Mitchell College of Law.

MARCIA AMIDON LUSTED

Marcia Amidon Lusted has written more than 160 books and 600 magazine articles for young readers. She is also an editor and works in sustainable development. She has traveled all over the world.